SIC FROM THE STAR WARS TRILOGY

SPECIAL EDITION

THE STAR WARS TRILOGY

This Edition contains the new compositions
VICTORY CELEBRATION by John Williams
JEDI ROCKS™ by Jerry Hey
From the *Return of the Jedi Special Edition*

T0057339

EXCLUSIVELY DISTRIBUTED BY
HAL•LEONARD®

Project Manager: Sy Feldman
Art Layout: Joann Carrera

Special Thanks to Michael Matessino, Nick Redman,
Sue Rostoni and Lucy Autrey Wilson.

CONTENTS

STAR WARS

THE EMPIRE STRIKES BACK

RETURN OF THE JEDI

From the Lucasfilm Ltd. Productions "STAR WARS", "THE EMPIRE SRIKES BACK"
and "RETURN OF THE JEDI" - Twentieth Century-Fox Releases.

STAR WARS
(Main Theme)

Music by
JOHN WILLIAMS

Star Wars - 2 - 1

From the Lucasfilm Ltd. Production "STAR WARS" - A Twentieth Century-Fox Release.

CANTINA BAND

Music by
JOHN WILLIAMS

8

From the Lucasfilm Ltd. Production "STAR WARS" - A Twentieth Century-Fox Release.

BEN'S DEATH/TIE FIGHTER ATTACK

Music by
JOHN WILLIAMS

Faster (♩ = 124)

Ben's Death/Tie Fighter Attack · 9 · 3

14

"Tie Fighter Attack"

Moderately fast (♩ = 140)

Ben's Death/Tie Fighter Attack - 9 - 7

Ben's Death/Tie Fighter Attack - 9 - 9

From the Lucasfilm Ltd. Production "STAR WARS" - A Twentieth Century-Fox Release.

PRINCESS LEIA'S THEME

Music by
JOHN WILLIAMS

With a Gentle Flow and Straight Eighth Feeling

Princess Leia's Theme - 2 - 1

From the Lucasfilm Ltd. Production "STAR WARS" - A Twentieth Century-Fox Release.

THE THRONE ROOM

Music by
JOHN WILLIAMS

Maestoso

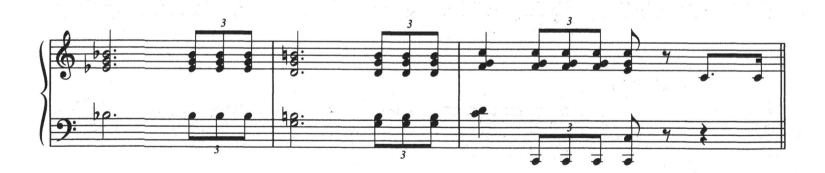

The Throne Room - 3 - 1

From the Lucasfilm Ltd. Production "THE EMPIRE STRIKES BACK"
- A Twentieth Century-Fox Release.

HAN SOLO AND THE PRINCESS

Music by
JOHN WILLIAMS

Han Solo and the Princess - 3 - 1

From the Lucasfilm Ltd. Production "THE EMPIRE STRIKES BACK"
- A Twentieth Century-Fox Release.

THE IMPERIAL MARCH
(Darth Vader's Theme)

Music by
JOHN WILLIAMS

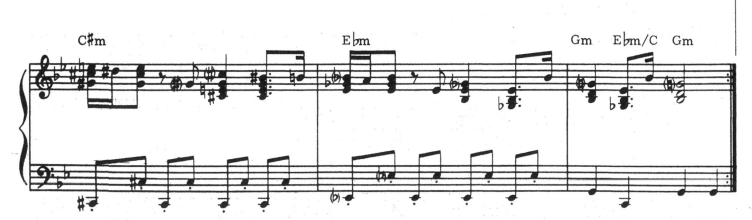

The Imperial March - 2 - 1

The Imperial March - 2 - 2

From the Lucasfilm Ltd. Production "THE EMPIRE STRIKES BACK"
- A Twentieth Century-Fox Release.

YODA'S THEME

Music by
JOHN WILLIAMS

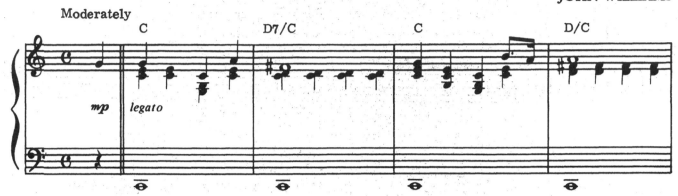

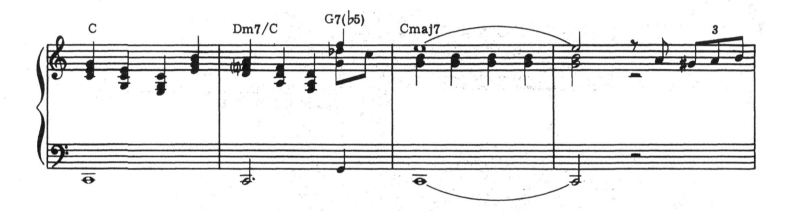

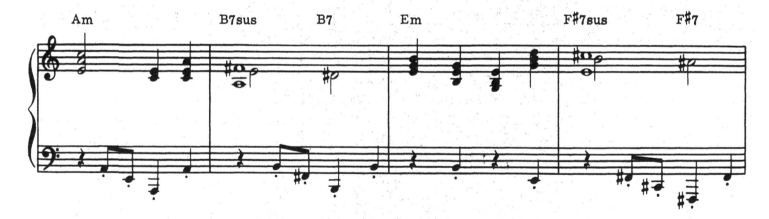

Yoda's Theme - 3 - 1

Yoda's Theme - 3 - 2

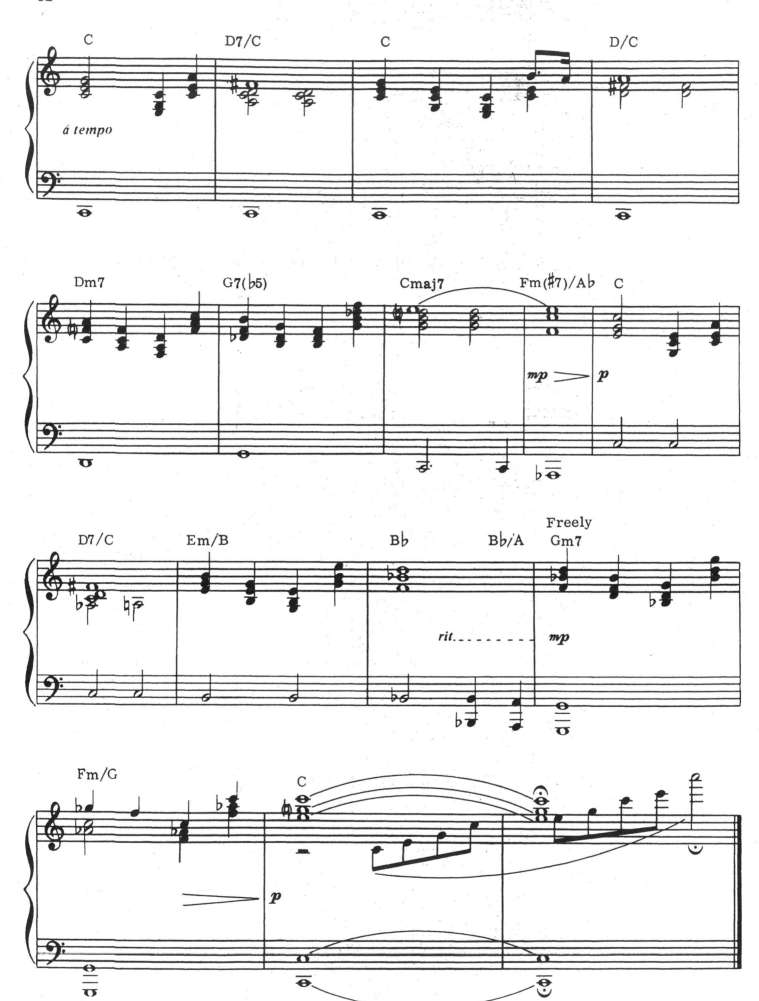

From the Lucasfilm Ltd. Production "THE EMPIRE STRIKES BACK"
A Twentieth Century-Fox Release.

MAY THE FORCE BE WITH YOU

Music by
JOHN WILLIAMS

May the Force Be with You - 2 - 1

May the Force Be with You - 2 - 2

From the Lucasfilm Ltd. Production "RETURN OF THE JEDI" - A Twentieth Century-Fox Release.

LUKE AND LEIA

Music by
JOHN WILLIAMS

Luke and Leia - 5 - 1

Luke and Leia - 5 - 3

Broadly

ff

Luke and Leia - 5 - 5

From the Lucasfilm Ltd. Production "RETURN OF THE JEDI" - A Twentieth Century-Fox Release.

PARADE OF THE EWOKS

Music by
JOHN WILLIAMS

Parade of the Ewoks - 6 - 1

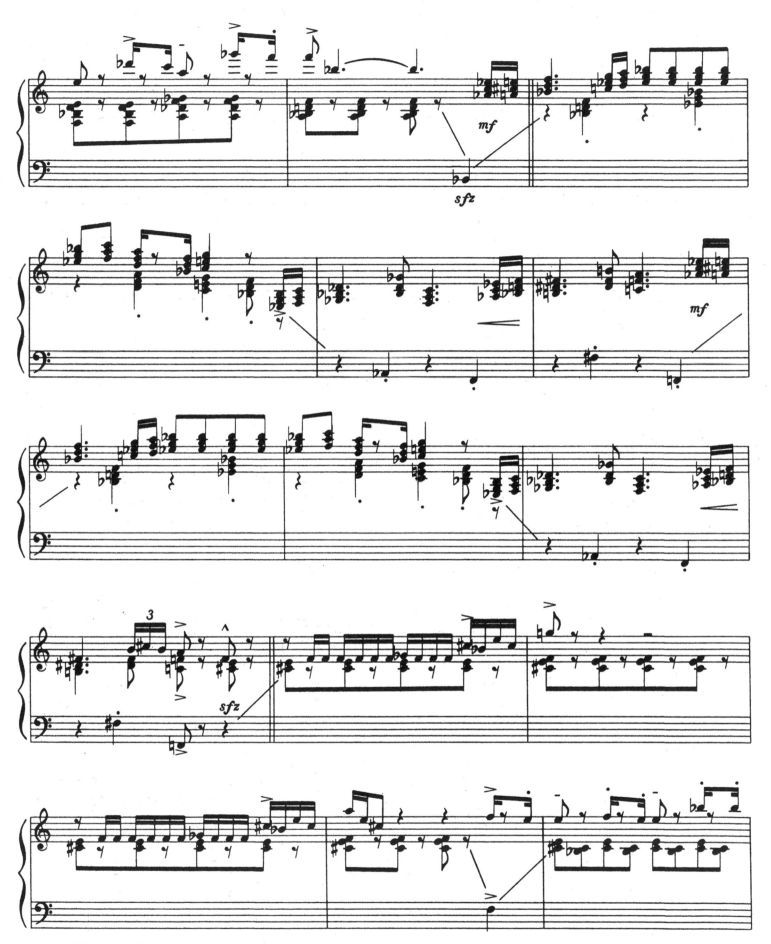

Parade of the Ewoks - 6 - 4

Parade of the Ewoks - 6 - 6

From the Lucasfilm Ltd. Production "RETURN OF THE JEDI"
- A Twentieth Century-Fox Release.

THE EMPEROR ARRIVES

Music by
JOHN WILLIAMS

The Emperor Arrives - 2 - 1

From RETURN OF THE JEDI SPECIAL EDITION

VICTORY CELEBRATION

Music by
JOHN WILLIAMS

From RETURN OF THE JEDI SPECIAL EDITION

JEDI ROCKS™

Music by
JERRY HEY

Jedi Rocks™ - 5 - 1

(Instrumental solo)